BASEBALL SMARTS

WHAT DOES AN
OUTFIELDER
DO?

Paul Challen

PowerKiDS
press™

New York

Published in 2017 by The Rosen Publishing Group, Inc.
29 East 21st Street, New York, NY 10010

Cataloging-in-Publication Data
Names: Challen, Paul.
Title: What does an outfielder do? / Paul Challen.
Description: New York : PowerKids Press, 2017. | Series: Baseball smarts | Includes index.
Identifiers: ISBN 9781499432855 (pbk.) | ISBN 9781499432879 (library bound) | ISBN 9781499432862 (6 pack)
Subjects: LCSH: Fielding (Baseball)--Juvenile literature. | Outfielders (Baseball)--Juvenile literature.
Classification: LCC GV870.C53 2017 | DDC 796.357'25--dc23

Developed and Produced for Rosen by BlueAppleWorks Inc.
Managing Editor for BlueAppleWorks: Melissa McClellan
Art Director: Tibor Choleva
Designer: Joshua Avramson
Photo Research: Jane Reid
Editor: Marcia Abramson

Photo Credits: Cover left Action Sports Photography/Shutterstock; cover right Fuse/Thinkstock; page tops Photology1971/Shutterstock; title page middle, p. 11 Eric Broder Van Dyke/Dreamstime.com; page bottoms Iasha/Shutterstock; TOC David Lee/Shutterstock; page backgrounds bottom Shawn Zhang /Shutterstock; page backgrounds top Eric Broder Van Dyke/Shutterstock; p. 4 Ffooter/Shutterstock; p. 5, 24, 28 Joseph Sohm/Shutterstock.com; p. 6, 10, 15 right, 23 Aspen Photo/Shutterstock.com; p. 7 left Michael Mitchell/Dreamstime; p. 7 right Michael Mitchell/Shutterstock; p. 8 Freddy Arenas/Dreamstime.com; p. 9 Matt_Brown/iStockphoto; p. 12, 18 Aspenphoto/Dreamstime.com; p. 13 Photographerlondon/Dreamstime.com; p. 14 tammykayphoto/Shutterstock; p. 15 left Derrick Neill/Dreamstime.com; p. 16 Mary Katherine Wynn/Dreamstime.com; p. 17 tomprout/iStockphoto; p. 19 Louis Horch/Dreamstime.com; p. 20 Keith Allison/Creative Commons; p. 22 Arturo Pardavila III /Creative Commons; p. 25 Lifesizelmages/iStockphoto; p. 26 left Keith Allison/Creative Commons; p. 26 right Keeton10/Dreamstime.com; p. 27 left Johnmaxmena2 /Creative Commons; p. 27 right Tim Warner/Keystone Press; p. 27 top Jerry Coli/Dreamstime.com; p. 29 Christopher Futcher/iStockphoto; back cover Eugene Onischenko/Shutterstock

Manufactured in the United States of America
CPSIA Compliance Information: Batch #BW17PK For Further Information contact: Rosen Publishing, New York, New York at 1-800-237-9932

CONTENTS

THE BASEBALL TEAM

Baseball is an action-packed sport played by two teams. There are nine players on a side, and games are divided into innings. Teams switch between offense and defense each inning. On the offensive side, a team tries to hit the ball and score runs. On the defensive side, teams try to stop their opponents from scoring using pitching, catching, and throwing.

On defense, a team is made up of a pitcher, infielders, outfielders, and a catcher. The pitcher and catcher combine to try to fool batters with pitches. Infielders position themselves close to home plate and try to field hit balls that come their way. Outfielders are farther away from home plate and try to catch balls hit to them.

Left Fielder

Outfield

Center Fielder

Right Fielder

Shortstop

Second Baseman

Third Baseman

Second Base

Third Base

Pitcher

Pitcher's Mound

First Baseman

Infield

First Base

Home Plate

Catcher

4

Because outfielders are the farthest defensive players from home plate, their main job is to catch deeply hit balls. Often, these are **fly balls** hit in the air without bouncing on the field itself. Outfielders have to cover a lot of ground, but they do often have more time to track down balls than their teammates in the infield.

The three outfield positions are right field, left field and center field. These three players have to work as a unit and must always communicate with one another, and with the rest of the team. They must also know how to position themselves behind the infielders so that their team covers the maximum amount of the field.

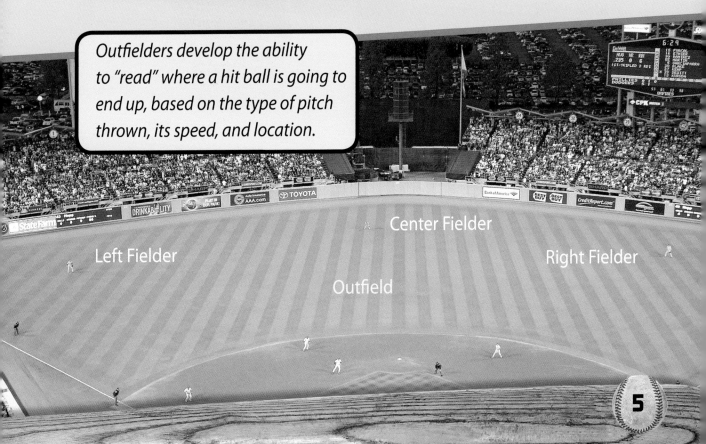

Outfielders develop the ability to "read" where a hit ball is going to end up, based on the type of pitch thrown, its speed, and location.

Center Fielder

Left Fielder

Right Fielder

Outfield

THE CATCH

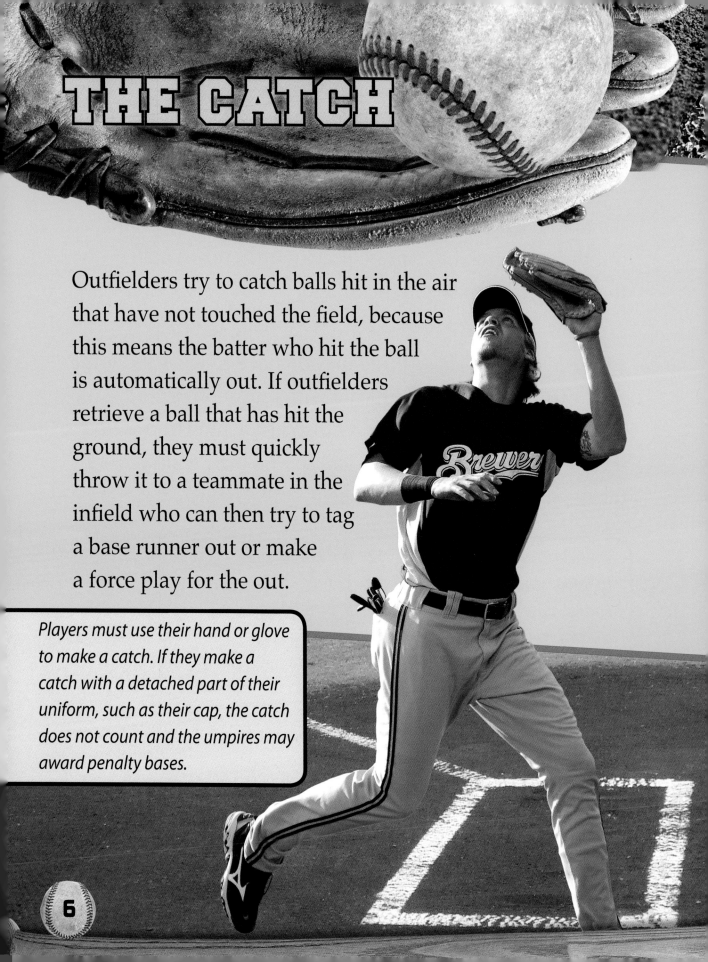

Outfielders try to catch balls hit in the air that have not touched the field, because this means the batter who hit the ball is automatically out. If outfielders retrieve a ball that has hit the ground, they must quickly throw it to a teammate in the infield who can then try to tag a base runner out or make a force play for the out.

Players must use their hand or glove to make a catch. If they make a catch with a detached part of their uniform, such as their cap, the catch does not count and the umpires may award penalty bases.

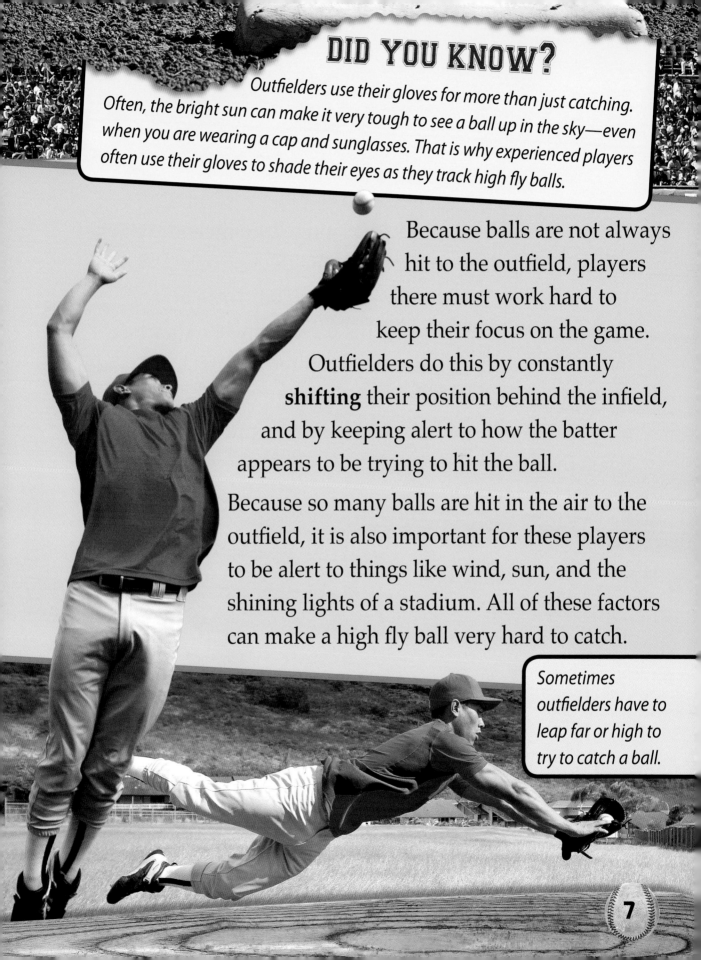

Because balls are not always hit to the outfield, players there must work hard to keep their focus on the game. Outfielders do this by constantly **shifting** their position behind the infield, and by keeping alert to how the batter appears to be trying to hit the ball.

Because so many balls are hit in the air to the outfield, it is also important for these players to be alert to things like wind, sun, and the shining lights of a stadium. All of these factors can make a high fly ball very hard to catch.

Sometimes outfielders have to leap far or high to try to catch a ball.

STRATEGY

When the ball is hit, outfielders judge its path and try to get to it as fast as they can. Smart outfielders can get a "jump" on a hit ball by knowing where it is likely to be hit and taking a few quick steps in that direction when they hear the crack of the bat. If the play requires a throw to be made after the catch, the outfielder needs a smooth motion to transfer the ball from glove to hand. Accuracy is also crucial when throwing to the infield.

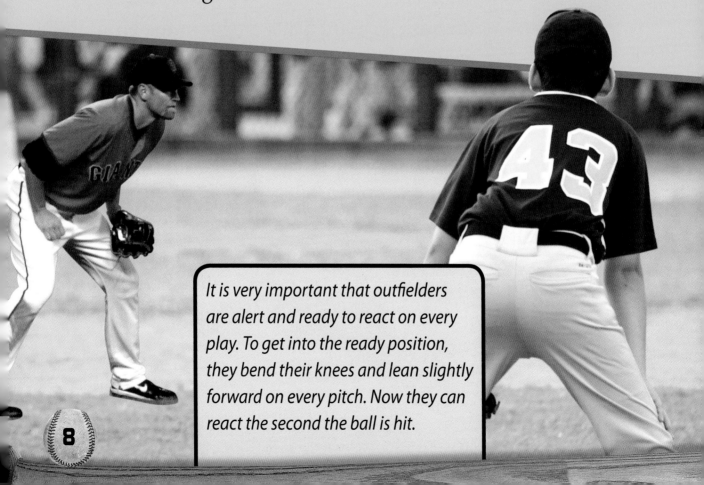

It is very important that outfielders are alert and ready to react on every play. To get into the ready position, they bend their knees and lean slightly forward on every pitch. Now they can react the second the ball is hit.

The three outfield players combine to shift positions for every batter. Right-handed and left-handed batters **pull** the ball to one side differently when trying to hit for distance, so outfielders have to be aware of this.

When tracking down a hit, an outfielder must quickly decide what will happen once they get the ball. Sometimes, a throw must go straight to a player covering an infield base. If the ball needs to go all the way to home plate, the distance may mean that the outfielder must throw to a cutoff player who will catch it and then throw it home.

Outfielders must be aware of how batters hit pitches thrown inside and outside the strike zone, as this can also determine where hits will go.

LEFT FIELDER

Because many batters are right-handed and pull deep balls to left field, the left fielder has to have good fielding and catching skills. Left fielders don't need the strongest arm in the outfield because they throw the ball a shorter distance to hold runners on base. That doesn't mean their arms are weak—they still can make bullet throws to home plate. They also need good judgment to patrol their section of the outfield.

Left fielders need speed and agility to make plays like this sliding catch. They often have a low error rate.

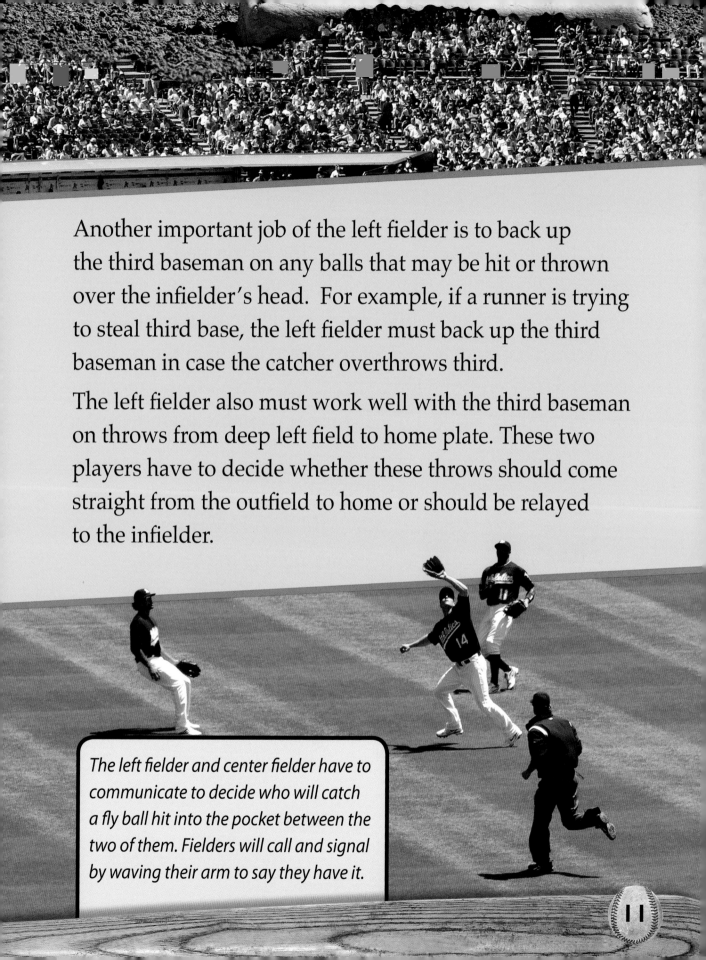

Another important job of the left fielder is to back up the third baseman on any balls that may be hit or thrown over the infielder's head. For example, if a runner is trying to steal third base, the left fielder must back up the third baseman in case the catcher overthrows third.

The left fielder also must work well with the third baseman on throws from deep left field to home plate. These two players have to decide whether these throws should come straight from the outfield to home or should be relayed to the infielder.

The left fielder and center fielder have to communicate to decide who will catch a fly ball hit into the pocket between the two of them. Fielders will call and signal by waving their arm to say they have it.

CENTER FIELDER

Of the three players in the outfield, the center fielder is usually the fastest and the one who covers the most ground. In fact, it is common for the center fielder to be the fastest player on a baseball team. Being able to catch on the run, quickly and accurately judge the flight of a ball, and react almost instantly when a ball is hit are valuable qualities in a center fielder.

It is also very helpful for a center fielder to have a powerful, accurate throw, because center field is the farthest distance from the infield.

Center fielders are responsible for covering the most territory because they are expected to back up the other two outfielders in case they miss a ball.

THE CAPTAINS

The center fielder is often considered the "captain" of the outfield. Because this player is in the middle of the three outfielders, the center fielder has to coordinate who will take responsibility for covering a fly ball, and who will back that player up. Center fielders need to know how to call off the other outfielders if they are confident they have the best chance to make a catch on a fly ball.

Often, center fielders are the most athletic players on a team—and this can mean they are great hitters as well.

Outfielders' speed makes them effective base runners, and over the years center fielders have become known as players who have good batting averages and can also steal bases.

RIGHT FIELDER

Like all outfielders, the right fielder needs to be fast and agile. Often, the player in this position is a stronger thrower than the player in left field, because a throw from right field to third base (a common play) must travel a long distance.

Backing up first base is a crucial skill for a right fielder as well. Balls thrown to the first baseman for force-outs or pickoffs from pitchers trying to catch base stealers leading off from first can sail over the bag, meaning the right fielder needs to be alert for those errant throws.

Right fielders do not need as much speed as center fielders, but they can't be slow. They often run over to back up the center fielder, second baseman, or first baseman.

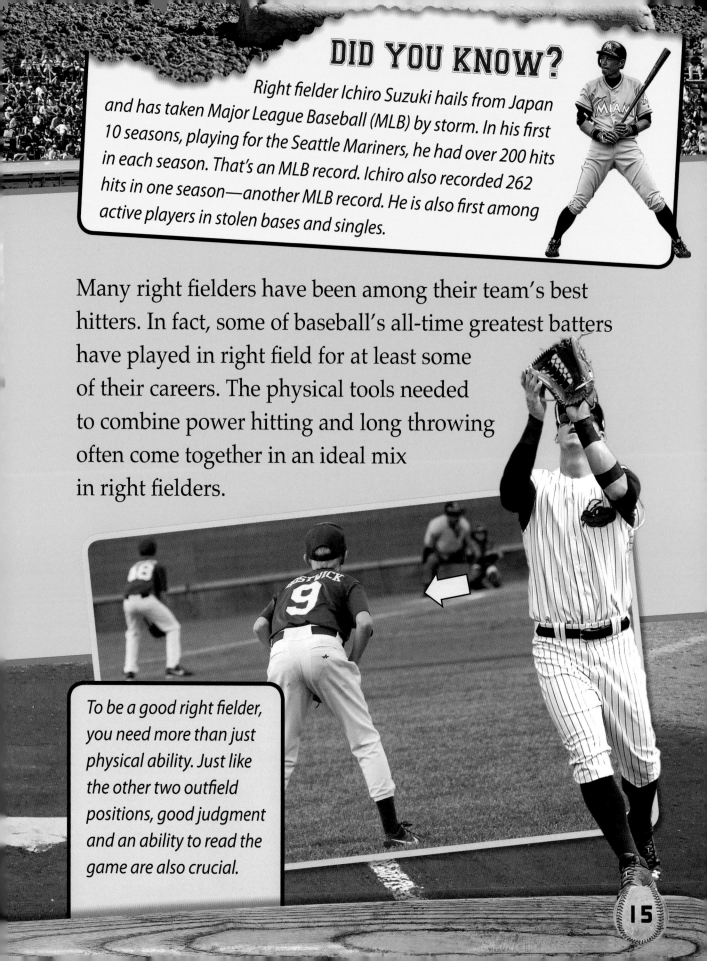

DID YOU KNOW?

Right fielder Ichiro Suzuki hails from Japan and has taken Major League Baseball (MLB) by storm. In his first 10 seasons, playing for the Seattle Mariners, he had over 200 hits in each season. That's an MLB record. Ichiro also recorded 262 hits in one season—another MLB record. He is also first among active players in stolen bases and singles.

Many right fielders have been among their team's best hitters. In fact, some of baseball's all-time greatest batters have played in right field for at least some of their careers. The physical tools needed to combine power hitting and long throwing often come together in an ideal mix in right fielders.

To be a good right fielder, you need more than just physical ability. Just like the other two outfield positions, good judgment and an ability to read the game are also crucial.

15

CATCHING THE BALL

Being able to catch a baseball may be the most important skill an outfielder needs to succeed. Lots of speed and even the ability to anticipate where a ball is going to be hit are not much use if a player is not actually able to make a catch.

On fly balls and **line drives**, the outfielder must work hard to get as close to the ball as possible as it flies through the air, following the ball right into a wide-open glove to make sure the ball does not bobble out.

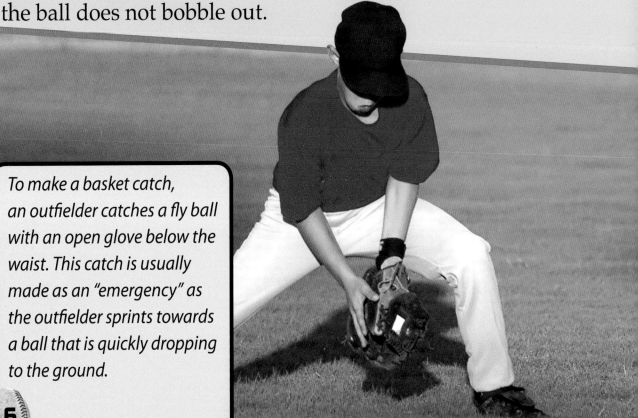

To make a basket catch, an outfielder catches a fly ball with an open glove below the waist. This catch is usually made as an "emergency" as the outfielder sprints towards a ball that is quickly dropping to the ground.

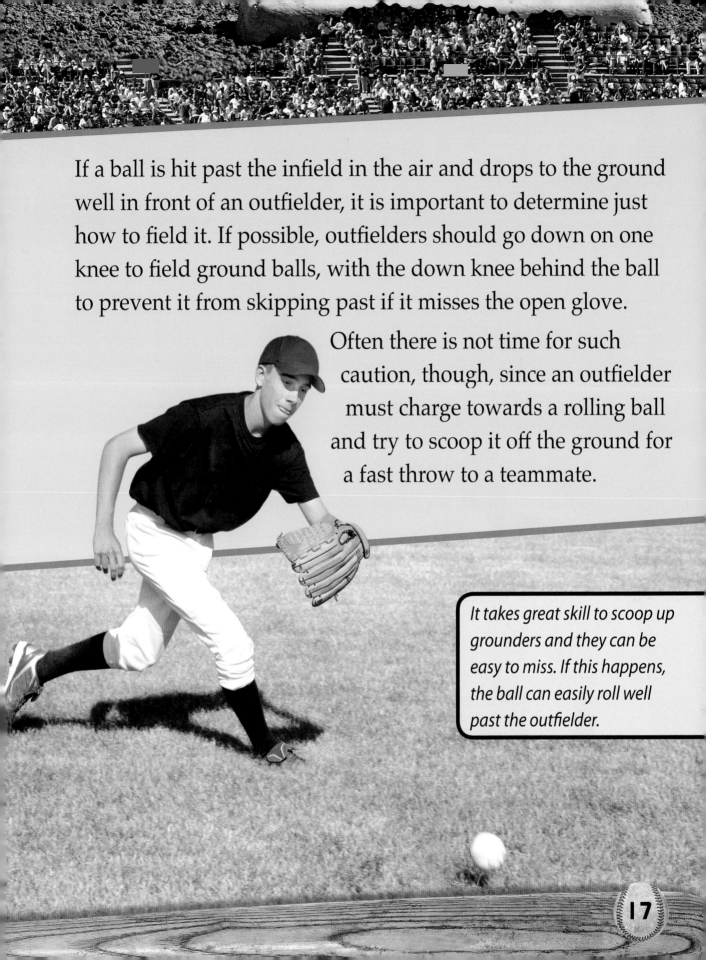

If a ball is hit past the infield in the air and drops to the ground well in front of an outfielder, it is important to determine just how to field it. If possible, outfielders should go down on one knee to field ground balls, with the down knee behind the ball to prevent it from skipping past if it misses the open glove.

Often there is not time for such caution, though, since an outfielder must charge towards a rolling ball and try to scoop it off the ground for a fast throw to a teammate.

It takes great skill to scoop up grounders and they can be easy to miss. If this happens, the ball can easily roll well past the outfielder.

THROWING THE BALL

Because the outfielder is so far away from home plate and the rest of the infield, long throws are an important part of this player's game. Of course arm strength is very important when making long, accurate throws, but so is proper throwing technique. The best outfielders use a smooth motion with a good follow-through to prevent the ball from tailing off as it gets closer to its target. Outfielders also need strong legs to be able to throw well.

A forceful step toward the ultimate target will make sure the throw has enough power to get there and will ensure accuracy.

When an outfielder cannot throw all the way to an intended base, it is important for a teammate to act as a cutoff. This means that a player must take up a position somewhere in or near the infield, to be able to catch a ball thrown by an outfielder. The cutoff player must then throw the ball to the necessary base.

Because the cutoff player has his back turned to the action in the infield, other players and coaches must yell instructions about where to throw next.

*Teams practice **cutoff plays** over and over to make sure they communicate well and know which bases to throw to in every possible situation.*

SPECTACULAR CATCHES

Baseball fans love to see home runs, but those who like the defensive side of the game also get a thrill when an outfielder denies a hitter of a homer! Outfielders who anticipate a well-hit ball can take off after it, running a route that gets them to the ball just before it flies over the wall. Often, stealing a home run involves jumping at just the right time, and extending the glove as far as possible to pluck the ball out of the air before it leaves the park.

When stealing a home run, outfielders have to be careful, since smashing into the outfield wall when trying to make a catch can lead to serious injury.

DIVING CATCHES

Diving catches are also an exciting part of the game. Since a ball that hits the ground is not an automatic out, many outfielders try to dive, headfirst with glove extended, to grab the ball before it hits the field.

Judgment is very important when making a diving catch. If the outfielder fails to nab the ball, it can easily roll well past the player who is sprawled on the ground, allowing the hitter to take extra bases. Sometimes outfielders must judge when not to make a catch. If a long fly ball goes foul with a runner on base, it may be safer to let the ball drop outof play and not risk trying to throw the runner out.

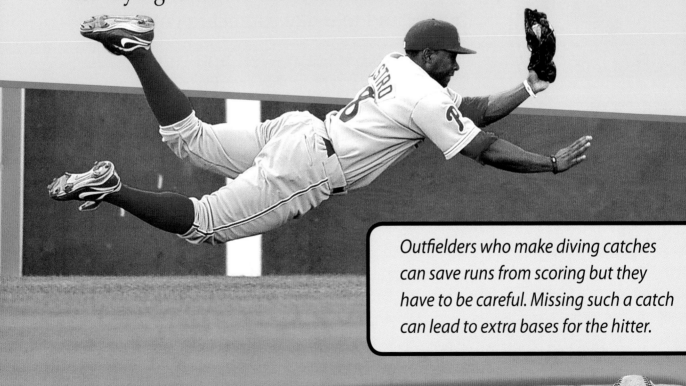

Outfielders who make diving catches can save runs from scoring but they have to be careful. Missing such a catch can lead to extra bases for the hitter.

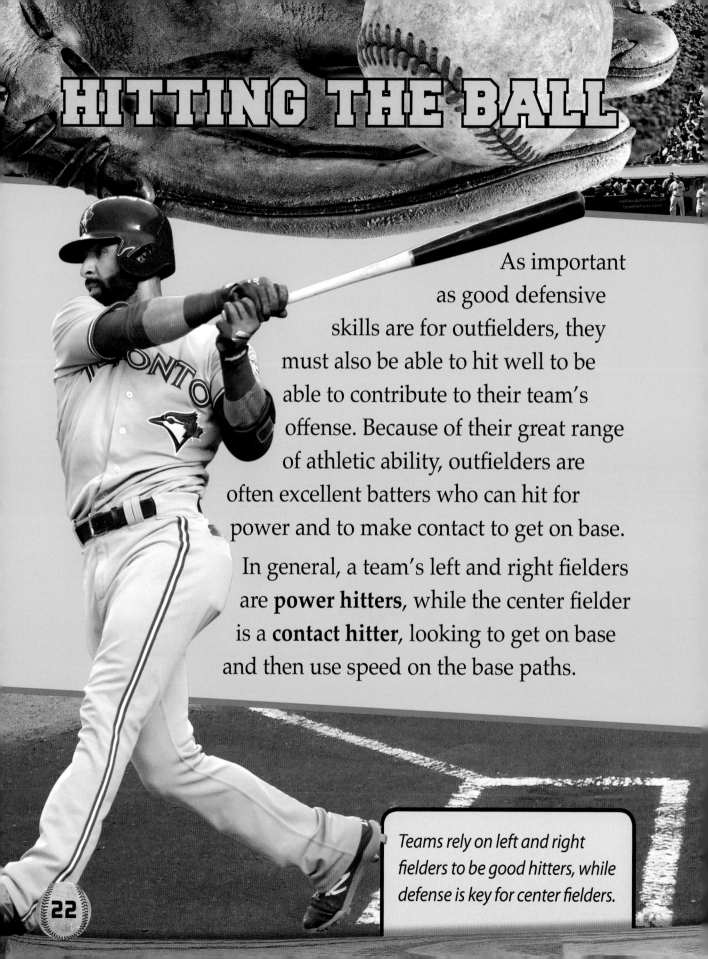

HITTING THE BALL

As important as good defensive skills are for outfielders, they must also be able to hit well to be able to contribute to their team's offense. Because of their great range of athletic ability, outfielders are often excellent batters who can hit for power and to make contact to get on base.

In general, a team's left and right fielders are **power hitters**, while the center fielder is a **contact hitter**, looking to get on base and then use speed on the base paths.

Teams rely on left and right fielders to be good hitters, while defense is key for center fielders.

It is impossible for three outfielders to cover all that ground between them, and the distance between the center fielder and the right or left fielder is known as the "gap" or the "alley." Hitters are always trying to hit the ball into these gaps, so outfielders need to be aware of this and must adjust themselves for maximum coverage.

STANCE

Like all players, outfielders need a sound batting stance to be successful at the plate. There are lots of different batting stances, but the basic body positioning is always the same: feet placed far enough apart for good balance, some bend in the knees, and hands together as they grip the bat.

Most good hitters start by placing a bit more weight on their back foot before shifting weight forward as they swing the bat. Keeping your balance is the key to a good stance, because it is easy to topple over when you are putting all your energy into a mighty swing.

Wandering pitches and foul tips may hit and even injure batters. For safety, they wear helmets and batting gloves. Some also put on elbow pads and shin guards, especially after an injury.

23

THE ROLE OF A MANAGER

One member of a baseball team never actually catches, throws, or hits a ball during a game, but has a very important job. Known as the **manager**, this person is similar to the head coach in other sports, such as hockey, football, or basketball. The manager makes many decisions from inside the **dugout**, such as which players to put in the defensive positions on the field, who should pitch, and what order the batters on a team should hit.

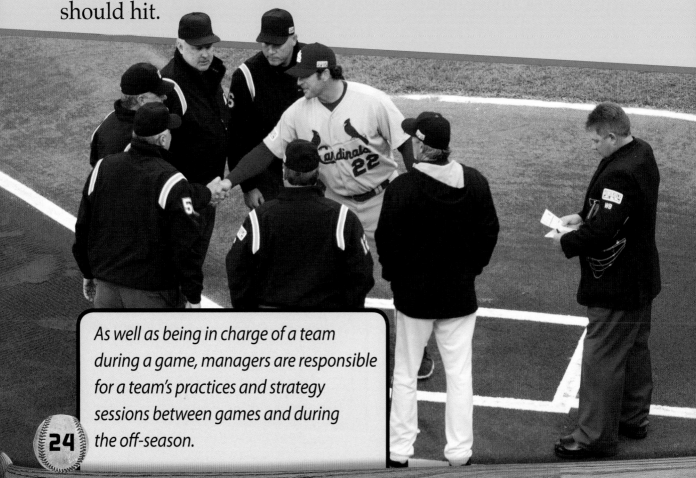

As well as being in charge of a team during a game, managers are responsible for a team's practices and strategy sessions between games and during the off-season.

COACHES ON THE FIELD

Managers are assisted by coaches who specialize in certain aspects of the game. Pitching coaches work with pitchers to hone their game, and hitting or batting coaches help offensive players work on their game behind the plate.

Coaches who work with outfielders help these players develop the skills they need to play in this position. They concentrate on tracking down long fly balls, long-distance throwing, and in-game strategy such as shifting and repositioning among the three outfield players to get ready for certain hitters.

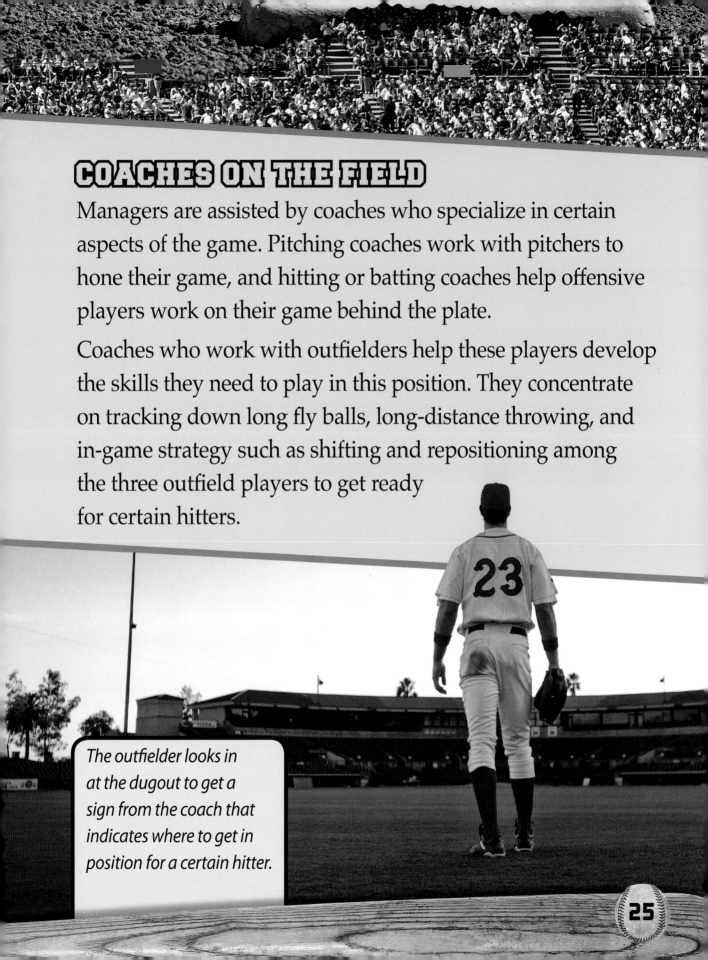

The outfielder looks in at the dugout to get a sign from the coach that indicates where to get in position for a certain hitter.

Some of baseball's all-time best players were outfielders. Powerful slugger Hank Aaron played 23 seasons in the major leagues between 1954 and 1976 and hit an amazing 755 home runs. Center fielder Ken Griffey Jr. had a 22-year career in the majors, hit 630 homers, and won 10 Gold Glove awards as the best center fielder in his league. Known as the "Yankee Clipper," Joe DiMaggio played 13 years in center field for the New York Yankees and hit safely in 56 straight games in 1941, a record that still stands.

Bryce Harper (left) of the Washington Nationals was 2012 Rookie of the Year in the National League (NL), tied for the most runs in the NL in 2015, and was voted the league's Most Valuable Player (MVP).

Andrew McCutchen (right) of the Pittsburgh Pirates made five straight All-Star games between 2011-15, and in 2013 was the MVP of the NL.

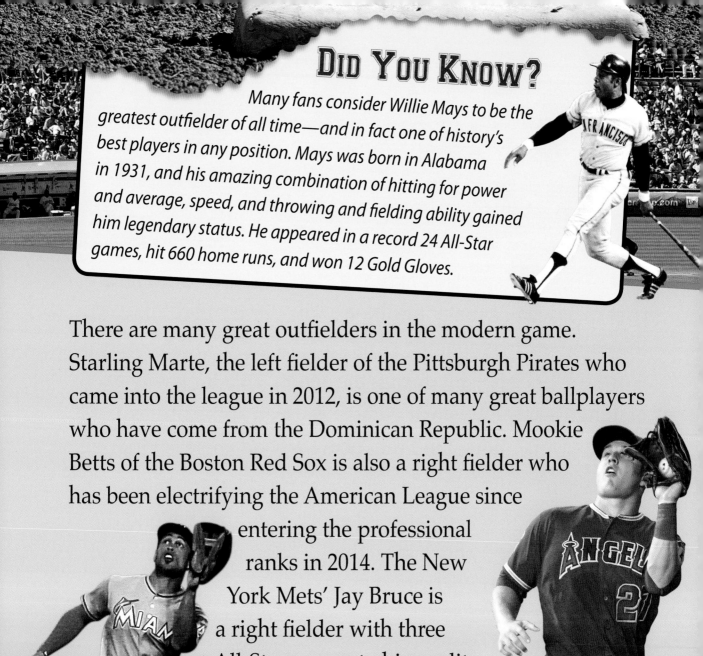

There are many great outfielders in the modern game. Starling Marte, the left fielder of the Pittsburgh Pirates who came into the league in 2012, is one of many great ballplayers who have come from the Dominican Republic. Mookie Betts of the Boston Red Sox is also a right fielder who has been electrifying the American League since entering the professional ranks in 2014. The New York Mets' Jay Bruce is a right fielder with three All-Star games to his credit.

Giancarlo Stanton (left) of the Miami Marlins is a right fielder and three-time major league All-Star.

Mike Trout (right) of the Los Angeles Angels of Anaheim has been selected MVP of the All-Star Game, and has made five appearances in it.

BE A GOOD SPORT

Fair play, good sportsmanship, and respect for the game are part of baseball's many traditions. The "unwritten rules" of the game, such as shaking hands after a game or a friendly word for an opponent during the action, go a long way to making baseball the great game it is. Even at the professional level, players understand that being a good sport is vital.

Coaches, parents, and spectators also need to remember the importance of being a good sport. This goes beyond the baseball diamond and is something everyone involved with baseball should participate actively in.

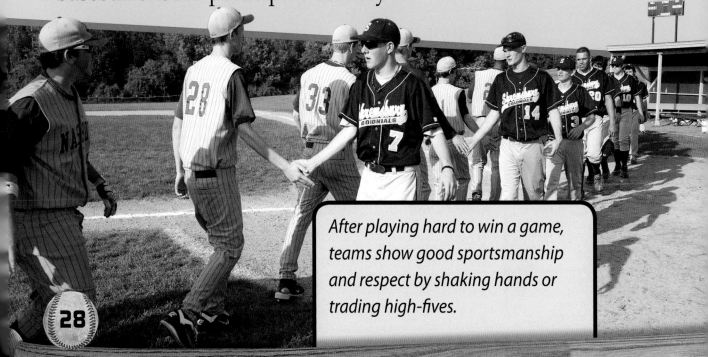

After playing hard to win a game, teams show good sportsmanship and respect by shaking hands or trading high-fives.

RESPECTING THE UMPIRE

Umpires want to call the best game they can, but because they must make hundreds of decisions every game, and because they are human, umpires can make mistakes. Players, coaches, and parents must remember this and respect the decisions umpires make, regardless of whether or not they seem correct. Failing to respect an umpire can ruin the game for everyone!

Because sometimes a lot of the action does not come their way, outfielders can stay safe by concentrating and being alert at all times during a game. Being aware of where the ball is—and when it is coming in your direction—can go a long way towards avoiding injury.

As well, the right equipment, a good diet, and a commitment to physical fitness are big factors in staying safe and enjoying the game to its fullest.

Baseball is all about a safe, fun, and competitive environment where everyone wins!

29

GLOSSARY

contact hitter A batter who attempts primarily just to make contact with the ball as an attempt to get on base.

cutoff play A play in which an outfielder throws the ball from the outfield to a teammate who then relays it to another teammate covering a base.

dugout Two low shelters on either side of a baseball field, one for each team, where players and coaches stay when not on the field.

fly ball A ball hit in the air, usually a considerable distance upwards.

line drive A ball hit in the air, usually not far above the field of play.

manager The "head coach" of a baseball team.

power hitter A batter who attempts to hit long balls that fall for doubles, triples, and home runs.

pull (the ball) To attempt to hit a ball at an angle so that it "pulls" to left or right field.

sacrifice fly A play in which a batter hits a deep fly ball, sacrificing their at-bat so a base runner can tag up and try to score.

shifting A defensive strategy used by an outfield to move as a unit to anticipate the direction a batter will hit the ball.

FOR MORE INFORMATION

FURTHER READING

Kelley, K.C. *Baseball Superstars 2016*.
New York: Scholastic, 2016.

LeBoutillier, Nate. *The Best of Everything Baseball Book*.
Mankato, MN: Capstone Press, 2014.

Tavares, Matt. *Henry Aaron's Dream*.
Somerville, MA: Candlewick, 2015.

Winter, Jonah. *You Never Heard of Willie Mays?!*
New York: Schwartz & Wade, 2013.

WEBSITES

Due to the changing nature of Internet links, PowerKids Press has developed an online list of websites related to the subject of this book. This site is updated regularly. Please use this link to access the list:

www.powerkidslinks.com/bs/outfielder

INDEX